Opening doors

Writings by children of Ireland and Russia for the Pushkin Prizes

1991-1996

Foreword by the Duchess of Abercorn
Preface by Tom Mullins
Introduction by Martin Waddell
Edited by Ann McKay
Designed and illustrated by Marilyn McLaughlin

ARTS COUNCIL of Northern Ireland

Grant-aided by the Arts Council

ISBN 0 9529338 0 2

Published by
The Pushkin Prizes Trust
Omagh Business Complex
Gortrush Industrial Estate
Omagh
Co Tyrone
BT78 5LS
Northern Ireland

Tel: 01662 249494
Fax: 01662 249451

Contents

Foreword

To discover that each of us has a "voice" is an exciting and enlivening experience!

It was an exciting experience for me when, for the first time, I became aware that my ancestor Alexander Pushkin had the power to say things in a special way which not only touched people's lives but which also united them in a bond of collectively-shared feelings. For that reason I felt he would be an appropriate guiding spirit in a creative prize that I initiated in Ireland in 1987.

Pushkin lived life to the full. He experienced life with all his senses and faculties. From an early age he enjoyed putting pen to paper. He wove the entire fabric of his life into every existing literary form – short stories, poems short and long, plays, novels and even a novel in verse, not to mention volumes of scintillating letters. Although Pushkin said things in his own way, his voice spoke for the people of his land – people who were looking for a sense of their own "Russian-ness".

In Ireland literature is loved and respected as much as it is in Russia. That is one of the glories of Irish culture. The stories and poems in this book, written by the young people of Ireland, are a continuation of that heritage. These works reflect the reality of a dynamic new Ireland expressed with the energy, spontaneity, and freshly-minted originality of a world being shaped anew.

To be able to bring to life a moment in time in such a way that makes others feel that they are sharing it – be it happy or sad – fearful or hilarious – or just simply memorable – is a hallmark of good writing.

The pieces in this second collection of writings from the Pushkin Prizes are all stamped with that hallmark. They exemplify the breadth and vigour of the creative imagination in our midst.

The Duchess of Abercorn

Sacha Abercorn.

Acknowledgements

Martin Waddell, writer
Tom Mullins, Lecturer in Education, University College, Cork
Antonina Kosyakina, Teacher, St Petersburg
Kate O'Hanlon, English Adviser SELB
Anne McAuley, English Adviser NEELB
Graeme Thomson, English Adviser SEELB
Paddy Ward, English Adviser WELB
Linda Simpson, General Primary Adviser BELB
Shiela McCaul, Senior Education Officer, WELB
Harry Cheevers, District Schools Inspector, North Donegal
Eileen Kent, District Schools Inspector, South Donegal
The late Pat Lavin, District Schools Inspector, Sligo

Principals, teachers, pupils and parents of:
Adhamhnáin Naofa NS, Letterkenny, Co Donegal; Chapel Road PS, Derry / Londonderry; Convoy Joint NS, Convoy, Co Donegal; Dalkey School Project NS, Glenageary, Co Dublin; Darragh Cross PS,Saintfield, Co Down; Donaghadee PS, Co Down; Glebe NS, Donegal Town; Harberton Special School, Belfast; Hardy Memorial PS, Richhill, Co Armagh; Hazelwood Integrated PS, Newtownabbey; Headford NS, Kells, Co Meath; Kilbroney PS, Rostrevor, Co Down; Scoil Mhuire na gCnoc NS, Knock, Co Mayo; Limavady HS, Limavady; Mill Strand Integrated PS, Portrush; Model PS, Derry / Londonderry; Moyle NS, Newtowncunningham; Rockport Prep. School, Holywood; Royal & Prior Comprehensive, Raphoe, Co Donegal; School No 166, St Petersburg, Russia; School No 455, St Petersburg, Russia; Scoil Aodha Rua agus Nuala, Donegal Town; Scoil Cholmcille, Letterkenny; Scoil Cholmcille, Newtowncunningham, Co Donegal; Seaview PS, Belfast; Steelstown PS, Derry / Londonderry; St Columb's NS, Moville, Co Donegal; St Columba's College, Stranorlar, Co Donegal; St Columba's PS, Draperstown; St John's Convent PS, Coleraine; St John's PS, Derry; St John's NS, Shannon, Co Clare; St Killian's / Cross NS, Mullagh, Co Cavan; St Mary's College, Derry / Londonderry; St Theresa's PS, Enniskillen; Windmill Integrated PS, Dungannon, Co Tyrone

Preface

Learning to sing ourselves. . .

Words invite children in many ways. Firstly, words are sensuous, offering an endless variety of sounds for the ear and a constant variation in shape and texture for the tongue and the lips; children like to play with words, to savour, to touch, to rearrange. And when words join in language there is the fascination of tone and rhythm to be encountered. Children delight equally in the rhythms of nursery rhymes and advertising jingles, it doesn't matter what is being said, the charm lies in how it's being said.

But children also know that words have power. Words bestow a means of ordering their inner and outer worlds and relating to others. When a child hears a strange sound at night and fear turns the sound into a monster, if the sound can be named the monster retreats banished by the light of language. Furthermore, children's curiosity urges them into incessant questions and imagined answers; in that way language becomes a powerful trigger for thought, for wonder and for creating personal space.

It is by giving due recognition to these aspects of children's relationship with language that interesting creative written work can be motivated. But there is more; if the writing is to be successful in an aesthetic way then the children must also have a sense of shape and form. Children need to learn that writing is a game with rules, a craft with skills to be learnt, and that by trying to cope with this they can create something worthwhile.

All good writing seeks to maximise its impact by minimising the words used. The less words, the more accurate and authentic the choice of words, the better the final creation. Forging such simplicity, avoiding clichés, poeticisms and literary stances is not easy. But if children end up saying "My black terrier" rather than "My sooty-coloured canine pal", if they realise that flowers are not a more suitable subject for poetry than a pig then they have taken a significant step towards authentic writing.

In the writing contained here all these elements mentioned above are found in varying degrees. There is the obvious delight in playing with words present in the poetry, there is the feeling of power and liberation coming from the stories that challenge the mighty adult world and finally there is in many pieces that sense of authentic human experience rendered into a simple and memorable statement.

Many of these authors may never write so well again, some may continue to produce work of quality. But this is not relevant here. What matters is that a moment of experience, real or imagined, has been captured, shaped and celebrated. A creative process has run its course and has called something into being words just for the pleasure of doing it. If, as Rilke says "we sing ourselves into existence" then there are some voices worth listening to here. Moments of song like this deserve to be cherished and shared; this anthology does that.

Tom Mullins
Cork, Sept 1996

Introduction

An open door

I can see you
playing amongst yourselves
but not with me

This extract from Ben Green's poem "The locked door" strikes, for me, the keynote of this collection. I know that feeling, from my playground days, and who doesn't? But in a child's world even locked doors open, when someone has the magic words and says them in the right order. That is what Ben's poem succeeds in doing. Reading it, the locked door of my own childhood opened. I was in his mind, and I felt his pain.

Finding the right words to describe any emotion or experience isn't easy, but in my view most of these young writers have managed it. Putting the words in the right order is even more difficult, and here the achievement is as uneven as might be expected, but every one of these pieces is still a considerable achievement, given the age of the writers concerned. This collection is a door they have opened for us, into their worlds. Go through it. I think you may be surprised and startled by what you find inside.

Martin Waddell

The locked door

by Ben Green

Dalkey School Project National School
Co Dublin
Highly Commended
1995

I can see you
Playing among yourselves
But not with me.

I can see you
Passing notes around the class
But none ever come to me.

I can hear you
Shouting and laughing
But not with me.

I can hear you
Planning an outing to the town
But you don't invite me.

I plead with you
But never will you let me in.

ALL·ALONE·IN·THE·CLOAKROOM

Dancing Class

by Maria Gillespie
Scoil Cholmcille, Newtowncunningham
Co Donegal

She was dancing,
Dancing her heart out,
Getting all the attention,
I got none.
Tension between teacher and me all evening,
I was left to teach the beginners,
The set dance I dance with Noel,
Was danced by him alone,
Tears stung my eyes as I watched,
I fled to the toilets,
held back the tears,
No one noticed as I left.
I began to dance all alone in the cloakroom,
No one to watch,
Back in the hall
Everyone was still engrossed in her.
Noel danced the set dance again,
This time she danced it with him.
I watched motionless,
At last it was time to go.
Could I come Saturday to watch the beginners? . . .
I shook my head furiously fighting the tears.
Ran out slamming the door,
They must have thought I was spoilt.
I didn't care.
I was being left out,
In bed that night I cried silently.
I'd been in that class seven years,
Now I was being ignored, left out.
I was empty, envious, eaten with jealousy.
It was the day I will never forget.

The day my daddy tried to kill the pig

by James Kelly

St Columba's Primary School,
Straw, Draperstown, Co Derry / Londonderry
Highly Commended
1993

Daddy lived on a farm when he was a boy. We still live on the same farm on the mountain to this day. In those days the farmhouse was only a small homeplace. Now it is renovated. We live approximately four miles from the town, so, long ago they had to see to their own food. They had to grow crops. Horses were needed to plough the furrows. A lot of spade work was used.

They also had to rear animals. For instance, hens gave them eggs as well as making a great Sunday dinner! An animal which was a necessity in those days was the pig! Pigs supplied the family and neighbours with gammon, pork and bacon, so the killing of the pig was a big event in family life.

So that's what this story is all about – the day my Daddy tried to kill the pig! It was Springtime. Daddy was fourteen. Granda thought he was big enough now to do a man's work. Granda sent Daddy to kill the pig. My two uncles, Patrick and Barney were sent with him. Daddy felt nervous but he set off to do the job and do it well. He had with him a sledge hammer and a sharp knife. He remembered Granda's advice. "Hit the pig right between the eyes. Mind you give it a good bang and then slit the throat. That way the blood drains quickly and the bacon will taste better."

Daddy prepared. My uncles dragged the pig out of the byre, using a strong rope.

They held tight but the ignorance of that pig really showed! It pulled and tugged and struggled. Daddy steadied himself with his sledge hammer. Have you ever heard of a "futter"? Well a "futter" is someone who always gets things wrong. Daddy was one of them.

The pig was still struggling. It pulled its head from side to side. It was frantic! Daddy took careful aim. He missed. He hit the pig on the back. He panicked. He stuck the knife into the pig's throat. A pig's throat is thick with blubber. The knife didn't go through. The daft pig escaped. What a hullabaloo! There was the pig running round the yard with a knife in its throat and Daddy and my two uncles running after it. The blood was flying everywhere. I don't know who was in a worse state, the pig or Daddy.

Daddy, Uncle Barney and Uncle Patrick ran round the yard in circles after that great ignorant pig. Daddy said "Hey, boys, I'm in it deep now." He just knew that Granda would kill him for sure. He had made a mess of this first big job. So Barney got the rope. He made it into a slip knot. He managed to get it over the pig's neck again. He and his brother Patrick put the rope over a branch and pulled hard. Soon, as if it were a miracle, they got the pig into a tight position and it couldn't move. Daddy took the knife and slit its throat.

They waited. The rest of the blood finally ran out. It seemed like hours but at last the pig died.

Weeks later, Granda tasted the first bacon from Daddy's pig. He said "I told you, John, making the bacon is easy. This is the tastiest bacon I've ever eaten."

IF ONLY HE KNEW!

Norman the conqueror

by David Shaw

Seaview Primary School, Belfast
Highly Commended
1995

Envied by all pupils is Norman
Who dared to brave the trap-door
Down
Down
Down
Below the stage.

What did he find there?
Confiscated comics?
A secret laboratory?
Or a porthole to another dimension?

Norman likes to keep them guessing . .

Frustration

by Orla Doran

Chapel Road Primary School,
Derry/Londonderry
First Prize
1992

The day began normally. I went to school, but the bully of the class, whose name was Brenda, came across the playground and on her way she pushed me. I pushed her back. She hit me. I went for her again.

"Stand straight", the teacher said.

"Well. We'll settle this at lunch-time", Brenda whispered.

"I'll settle you, don't worry".

It irritated me that she would get away with starting fights. I sat in the class and did all my work even though my hand shook. I looked at my watch. It was 12.24. I was dreading the bell. I sat worried. 12.24. Lunch is at 12.30.
HOW CAN I FACE HER?
WHEN WILL I FACE HER?
WHERE WILL I FACE HER?
All these questions rang through my head. I stared across the class.

Brenda gave me dirty looks. "So what", I thought, "I'll beat her. She couldn't beat a fly."

Time past. Minutes seemed more like seconds. 12.29.

OH NO. I began to bite my nails. OH YOU CAN'T DO THIS TO ME, BELL. GO BACK AN HOUR. The bell rang. OH WHAT WILL I DO? I walked out of the classroom. I went to the hall and ate my lunch and went to the playground. Brenda was at the other end. I looked at her. She was tall with long brown hair. This was a really good advantage. She walked over and slapped me across the face. I slapped her. We began to really dig into each other. "Big scrap!", everyone shouted and ran towards us. I felt like killing her but she was bigger than me. What was I to do?

I had never been in a real fight before. As she grabbed for my hair, the Principal came and tore us apart. "You're for it, Brenda, I have given you a warning. Now your next step is out of this school", the Principal said.

"You're for it", Brenda threatened.

"I don't care", I said shrugging my shoulders.

The Principal made us promise we wouldn't fight any more. I was glad in one way but sorry as well. I think I really could have beaten her had I had the chance. Now I would never know except if she started something up again. I was glad too because I hate the idea of fighting and maybe, just maybe, she might have made mincemeat of me.

MAKING • MINCEMEAT

A quare bird around Derry

by Francesca Nic Colla

Bunscoil Bhaile Stil, Doire/
Steelstown Primary School, Derry/Londonderry
First Prize
1993

The trouble all began in school. The teacher was talking about flight long ago. I was reading about Amelia Earhart and Icarus. That started me thinking . . . If they can do it so can I!

There wasn't a minute to lose. I got paper and a pen. I'll need feathers and wax. What day will I do it? What time? Sunday before eleven o'clock Mass, is when I'll do it. I'll be stinking rich. John Major will give me money for being the first woman to fly solo over the Foyle!

At home I began to gather up the things I would need. Mum usually keeps three dozen candles in the press. Now there's none! She wouldn't miss a couple of candles - but I'm not so sure about a couple of dozen! And you should see Daddy's hens outside! They're all bald, however that happened! I'm ready.

On Sunday I listened to the weather forecast on the radio. "It will be very windy up round Derry" I went up to Grianan and it was certainly windy enough there. Great. I'll go to Altnagelvin. I jumped . . . I fell . . . I jumped . . . I fell . . . I jumped . . . I flew! Yippee! I was flying. My hands will be falling off me from signing autographs. No, I wasn't frightened at all. On behalf of the President of Ireland I would like to . . . suddenly I hit the cathedral. It was my first time up on the spire. That bell's terrible. Bong! Bong! Awful. If I put a few feathers round this part . . . There. It's stopped!

I flew on quickly but a bird came by. And then another and another. They started hitting my wings. "Get lost! Scram! Stop it," I said. "I'm the one that fed youse on the bird table." I started to fall.

I was above a school! I looked in a window. What's the Principal doing at school on a Sunday? Ooops! Time for me to fly!

I flew over some of the city. Several people started to shout and stare. Nosey busybodies! "The Brits in their latest plane," shouted one man. "IRA," exclaimed a boy. "UFO," said a young girl, "A Martian". A woman fainted. What's wrong with them? They didn't do this when Icarus started flying.

I headed off towards the bridge. I needed a rest by this time. Suddenly the RSPB arrived, they made a circle round me. There were people with cameras, others with tape recorders. I heard the click! click! The traffic had come to a standstill. A worm of cars trailed back as far as the Guildhall. I fell. I was in the water.

At this point two things happened. First there was a fishing competition taking place and . . . yes, you guessed it. I frightened all the fish away. And the second thing that happened was that I won the competition! The feathers fell off my arms but I had a big fat salmon in my mouth. Yes, I won the National Fishing Competition.

That night I was to go to the Mayor to receive my award. I was ready, my best clothes on me. I was right in the middle of the story (I was talking to my mother) when the lights went out. "Where are my candles?" she said. "Francesca, have you seen my candles? Francesca!"

And so that's how it happened. A girl who achieved all those wonderful things is now grounded for a month. Now if I could tie these sheets together and unlock the window (I've seen this done on the television), if I could do that and then climb over the wall . . .

Éan Corr Fá Dhoire

Le Francesca Nic Colla

atá ag freastal ar Bhunscoil Cholmcille,
iardhalta de chuid
Bhunscoil Bhaile Stíl, Doire.

Thosaigh an trioblóid uilig ar scoil. Bhí an múinteoir ag caint linn fá Amelia Earhart agus Icarus. Chuir sin ag smaoineamh mé . . . Má thig leosan é a dhéanamh, thig liomsa!

Ní raibh bomaite le cailleadh. Fuair mé páipéar agus peann. Beidh cléití agus céir de dhíth orm. Cén lá a dhéanfaidh mé é? Cén t-am?

Déanfaidh mé Dé Domhnaigh é roimh Aifreann a haon déag. Beidh mé an-saibhir. Tabharfaidh John Major duais airgid dom de thairbhe gur mé an chéad bhean le heitilt thar Abhainn an Fheabháil leí féin!

Sa bhaile thosaigh mé ag bailiú na rudaí a bheadh de dhíth orm. Triocha is a sé coinneál a bhíodh ag mo mháthair sa chófra. Níl ceann ar bith anois ann! Ní chaillfeadh Mamaí cúpla coinneál – ach cad é faoi cúpla dosaen! Agus da bhfeicfeá na cearca atá ag Daidí amuigh ansin! Achan ceann acu maol. (Cibé dóigh ar tharla sin!) Tá mé réidh.

Dé Domhnaigh, d'éist mé le Réamhfháisnéis na hAimsire ar an raidió.
"Beidh an lá iontach gaofar fá Dhoire". Chuaigh mé go dtí an Ghrianáin agus bhí sé gaofar go leor ansin. Sin go maith. Rachaidh mé go hAlt na Gealbháin. Léim mé . . . Thit mé . . . Léim mé . . . Thit mé . . . Léim . . . D'eitil mé! Yipee! Bhí me ag eitilt. Beidh mo lámha nimhneach ag síniú autographs. No, Ní raibh eagla ar bith orm. Thar

cionn Uachtarán na hÉireann ba mhaith liom . . . Go tobann bhuail mé an tArdeaglais. Ní raibh mé riamh ag an bharr. Tá an clog sin go dona! Bong! Bong! Tá sé millteanach. Má chuirim cuid de na cléití seo thart ar an phíosa sin . . . Sin é. Tá sé stopaithe!

D'eitil mé ar aghaidh go gasta ach tháinig éan. Agus ansin ceann eile agus ceann eile. Thosaigh siad ag bualadh mo chuid eiteoga. "Bígí ar shiúl! Scuit! Stadaigí sin," arsa mise. "Mise an duine a thug bia daoibh ar tabla na n-éan". Thosaigh mé ag titim.

Bhí mé ar bharr scoile! D'amharc mé isteach ar an fhuinneog. Cad é tá an Príomhoide ag déanamh ar scoil ar an Domhnach? Ooops! Tá an t-am agam a bheith ag imeacht!

D'eitil mé thar cuid den chathair. Thosaigh a lán daoine ag glaoch agus ag féachaint orm. Daoine fiosracha! "Sasanaigh in eitléan nua s'acu", arsa fear amháin.
"IRA", arsa gasúr.
"UFO", arsa girseach. "Duine ó Mars."
Thit bean i laige. Cad é tá cearr leo? Ní dhearna siad seo nuair a bhí Icarus ag eitilt.

D'imigh mé liom go dtí an droichead. Bhí scíste de dhíth orm fán am seo. Go tobann tháinig an R.S.P.B. Rinne siad ciorcal thart orm. Bhí daoine le ceamraí, daoine le téipthaifeadáin. Chuala mé an clic! clic! Bhí an trácht stopaithe. Bhí peist de charranna siar go dtí an Guild-hall. Thit mé. Bhí mé san uisce.

Ag an phointe seo tharla dhá rud. Bhí comórtas iasaireachta ar siúl agus . . . Sea, tá an ceart agat.

Scanraigh mé na héisc uilig. Agus an dara rúd a tharla ná gur bhain mé an comórtas! Thit na cléití uilig de mo lámha ach bhí bradán mór ramhar i mo bhéal agam. Sea, bhain mé Comórtas Náisiúnta Iascaireachta.

An oíche sin bhí mé le dul go dtí an Méara agus mo dhuais a fháil. Bhí mé réidh, na héadaí is fearr atá agam orm. Bhí mé go díreach i lár an scéil (ag caint le mo Mhamaí a bhí mé) nuair a d'imigh na soilsí.
"Cá bhfuil mo choinnlí?" ar sise.
"Francesca, an bhfaca tú mo choinnlí? A Francesca!"

Agus sin mar a tharla. Girseach a rinne na rudaí iontacha sin uilig anois sa teach, agus gan cead aici dul amach go cionn míosa. Anois dá dtiocfadh liom na braillíní a cheangail le chéile agus an glas a bhaint den fhuinneog. (Chonaic mé seo déanta ar an teilifís uair amháin), dá dtiocfadh liom sin a dhéanamh agus ansin dreapadh thar an bhalla . . .

Gran's dresser

Kerry Russell
Moyle National School, Newtowncunningham
Co Donegal

Highly Commended
1992

It stood in Gran's kitchen
Showing off all her delph,
Cups, bowls, and plates
Filled every shelf.

Even when I can't see it
It's there in my mind . . .
The good-sides faced outwards
And the cracks turned behind.

The plates edged with daisies
She'd bought in Kilkenny,
Twenty-five years ago
At a Fair, for a penny.

Each item displayed
Was a very great treasure,
Not for its worth
But just for its pleasure.

For the dresser was a book
And the delph its pages,
That carried Gran's story
Down through the ages –

A story of life,
Its joy and its sorrow
The hopes of today
And the fears of tomorrow.

An awful Saturday

by Siofra McSherry

St John's Convent Primary School,
Coleraine, Co Derry / Londonderry
Second Prize
1995

An Average Saturday Morning

"Ohhhhhhh . . . Mummy," I moaned. "You don't need another skirt!"

"Mmph . . ." she murmered vaguely. She twirled a navy, knee-length skirt around her legs. "What do you think?"

I gave up to the inevitable. "It's all right. I don't like the belt, though."

"No," she agreed slowly. "It is a little gaudy. But I can always use a different one."

A simpering, brown-haired girl stepped up to us. "Can I help you?" she enquired. I groaned inwardly. Now I'd never get out of 'Chic'!

By now Mummy was laden with black and navy knee-length skirts. "I'll have this one too," she was announcing to the world in general. She had put on her posh telephone voice. The girl was remarking how nice it looked and what good value etc, etc . . .

I was sitting on a wobbly cane chair reading Asterix. The chair (which was very uncomfortable) was situated under a low flight of stairs. I was cramped between a 'happy face' vacuum cleaner and a large carton of disinfectant. Even the jokes in 'Asterix' were a little dull. Mummy was in the changing room, trying on her skirts. Now and then she strutted out of the curtained room to ask my opinion. I was indifferent, but even I could see the skirts just weren't right.

After a period of strolling and opinion-asking, Mummy decided to buy two skirts. The simpering girl charged us thirty-five pounds. Apparently that was an amazing bargain.

As we left the shop, mummy cried out "Hello, dear!" to a passer-by.

I groaned. When Mummy started talking, she didn't stop.

I leaned against the metal-and-glass door to read. I was standing in a draught.

I shivered, and withdrew into the shop. Oh, well, we'd go to Crazy Prices Superstore soon and then we'd go home.

I settled down to wait. Mummy would probably make me help with cleaning at home, but it'd be better than shops.

Disaster Afternoon

An hour or so later, I knelt down in front of the kitchen cupboard. A strange assortment of bottles and cartons met my eyes. "Right," I mumbled. "Clean the bedroom, mirror, make beds, dusting, Mummy says. Right."

I rummaged for a duster. I exposed a long-forgotten dishcloth. "Archeologists' discovery of the year! Oldest household dishcloth!" I could almost read the headlines.

I supposed it would do. It was only a little dirty.

Now for Windowlene. 'Windows / mirrors, clean in a wipe!' A dusty spray-can appeared after some searching. I guessed it was Windowlene. It didn't really say.

I collected an aerosol that said: (Smudge) (Smudge) 'Shine like the sun'. It was probably furniture polish. I headed upstairs.

* * *

In my bedroom I glanced at my cleaning resources. I picked up the dishcloth and flicked it over the ornaments on my dressing table. At least they looked clean.

Now for the mirror, I picked the dirty spray can and squirted it experimentally over a corner and wiped it with the dish cloth. Dirt stuck all over the quivering mess, but it stayed on the mirror. Desperately I sprayed the aerosol all over the grime and wiped it. It removed the Windowlene but not the dirt.

I now had a soppy, wet dishcloth on my hands, as well as a dirty mirror. I held the dishcloth by its frayed damp corner and stretched it out in front of me. I began to walk towards the door intending to go to the bathroom. I opened the door . . . and tripped over the brass carpet joiner. The dishcloth flew across the hall and landed on a rose in the carpet pattern. I'm afraid I said something I shouldn't.

I scrambled for the bathroom. If I could live through . . .

I searched the room for a cloth. I found a wet sponge. I grabbed some scented pink soap, knocking over a tube of toothpaste. I stepped back and stood on the tube! It squirted all over the floor. I rushed back to the dishcloth. I scrubbed the dirty spot with the sponge and soap. An interesting pink foam appeared, making the carpet go white.

I gulped and tried to clean it with a crumpled tissue. The tissue stuck in little bits in the foam.

"Uh-oh", I said. "So much for Guardsman, 'stop a spill becoming a stain'".

When I grow up I won't half murder my children for doing their best.

Catty exercises

by Tracey Kerrigan

St Columb's National School,
Moville, Co Donegal
3rd Prize
1993

My black cat yawns,
Opens her jaws,
Stretches her legs
And shows her claws.

Up she gets,
And stands on four,
Long stiff legs
And yawns some more

Lifting her self
On her delicate toes
She arches her back
As high as it goes.

Letting her self down
With particular care,
She walks away
With her tail in the air.

The horrible statue

by Louise Beck

Mill Strand Integrated Primary School,
Portrush, Co Antrim
First Prize
1994

"Honey, I'm leaving for bingo now." Mum yelled as she splashed on more of her cheap makeup.

She always went to bingo on a Saturday night all dressed up, – high heels, makeup – anything that would make her look like a winner.

Mum, I'm afraid, was that kind of type, you know the ones that always drink tea and gossip to friends about what's in the latest women's magazine.

"Bye." I shouted back. "Make sure you win something." Looks like I said it all. Mum came back that night with the weirdest shaped box; it was black with white scotch tape wrapped round it.

"What you got there mum?" I asked.

"Oh, it's some sort of statue I won at bingo. Let's open it."

Mum slowly unwrapped the scotch tape and took off the box. I'd never seen such a horrible statue in all my life, it had the most frightening face, eyes like the devil and teeth like a vampire's.
"Oh, isn't it lovely. We'll have to put him somewhere everyone can see him." Mum smiled.

That night I kept on thinking about those eyes and the way mum thought it was so nice, I must have jumped up at least fifty times from my sleep.

Next morning mum was washing the statue in the bath, the black paint had started to come off and it had turned red. I ran into my bedroom and wrote on my blackboard THAT STATUE HAS GOT TO GO!

That's when Plan A went into action.

The first thing I had to do was get the statue out of parent reach, so I went back to the bathroom in my dressing up army suit and said in my sweetie-pie voice, "Mum you go put your feet up and I'll finish here."

"A boy cleaning a statue, well I suppose it's for a good cause, okay."

Mum walked off down the stairs picking up her Women's Weekly at the same time.

"Right, statue, stand to attention. You're in army camp now. Now I may be a small nine year old boy but I'm your sergeant and you'll do everything I say, understand."

The eyes of the statue just stood and stared.

"Looks like you're gonna be a toughie," I said crossly.

"Matthew hurry up with that statue. I want it outside as soon as possible," his mum shouted.

I quickly took the statue out of the bath and wrapped it in a towel, then I ran downstairs with it and slipped out the back door.

"This should be a good place where no one can see it."

I carried it over to the oak tree where it was nicely covered by the leaves.

"Well, that's it well hidden, now to just think of a way to get rid of it."

It was tea time when I came up with my brilliant idea.

"Mum, the bin lorry comes on Friday, doesn't it?" I asked

"Yes, why."

"It's just something I'm doing in school."

Friday morning.

"This is my chance to get rid of that stupid statue." I yelled.

I walked downstairs, got the statue, put it in a bin bag and just as I was going to put it with the rest of the rubbish mum came.

"What are you doing, Matthew?"

"Oh, just putting my rubbish in the bin."

"Okay." Mum said and walked back into the house.

When I completed my task I went into the kitchen and had breakfast.

"Matthew, you haven't seen my statue? I haven't seen it since Monday."

"No." I said with a grin on my face.

* * *

It was Bingo night. Mum was putting on all her gear.
Beep, Beep.

"There's the taxi, Mum."

"Oh right, bye."

When she came home that night she had a box and guess what.

IT WAS THE SAME ONE!

And that's when Plan B went into action.

My face

by John Woolsey

The Model Primary School,
Derry/Londonderry
Third Prize
1994

My face looks like an ancient map.
My nose resembles a mountain.
I can feel it sticking out a lot.
My wrinkles are old like sewage pipes underground.
My eyes are little lakes drifting from side to side.
My mouth is big like a volcano.
It smiles and can be unhappy.
My eyebrows are complicated forests of the deep.
They protect me in battle.
My hair is a parachute, it shelters me from the rain.
It protects me from the cold now that I am old.
My ears hear the cries of the living creatures
Protesting about pollution of the world.

Wonderful worlds?

by Roisin Martin

St Theresa's Primary School,
Enniskillen, Co Fermanagh
First Prize
1991

"Oh, shut up!" I yelled at my brother, who was scampering away, a wide grin on his face. "Grrr," I gritted my teeth. "Now, don't get so upset dear," said Aunt Marge, good-naturedly. "He's only a little boy." "Little, my foot," I thought, "more like scrawny!"

It was true: he was scrawny and untidy with grey eyes and a mouth that was nearly always open, yelling insults. He always wore a stupid baseball cap, scruffy jeans and some obscene T-shirt.

But I couldn't argue with Aunt Marge. Instead I stomped out of the house, down the road and into the forest. In the middle, evergreen trees gave way to a clearing, where clumps of brightly coloured flowers and plants bloomed and grass grew greener and fresher than anywhere else. Here lay fallen trees, now covered with moss and ivy, which blended into the background.

I sat on one of the fallen trees and sighed. I wished I was someone else. Someone unlike me. I was clumsy with stumpy legs and mousy-brown hair. I had dull brown eyes and a pointy nose. My clothes were always pretty boring and it seemed as if nothing remotely exciting had ever happened to me in my eleven years.

NOTHING • REMOTELY
EXCITING • HAD • EVER
HAPPENED • TO • ME

Suddenly, I felt a warmth against my shoulders and I looked up. A bright light glowed in front of me. All of a sudden it changed to a delicate, little figure with a snub nose and glistering, green eyes. Her hair was red and waistlength. She wore a long, white robe and her lily-white skin was adorned with a single, tiny star which was positioned on her forehead.

In her hand she held a bundle of items and as she laid them beside me, I recognised two of them. There were my Great Aunt Maud's spectacles, an expensive-looking diamond necklace and my headmistress' mortarboard.

The lady smiled at me and said "My name is Twilight and I am a good witch. If you wish to be someone else just place their item on your person and you immediately become her in body and mind." And so saying, Twilight vanished.

I decided to try out Great Aunt Maud's spectacles first. She was a sour lady who always wore a sharp expression and whose lips were always tightly pursed together. Her hair was snowy-white and tied in a tidy top-knot. As for her clothes, long, old fashioned dresses covered her dark, forbidding figure and in her hand she carried a long, wooden cane on which intricate designs were carved.

As soon as I placed her spectacles on my nose, I was changed. I was also standing in a completely different scene. Instead of the forest surrounding me there were high marble staircases and oaken furniture. "Mary!" I found myself calling in a high, hoarse voice and a maid appeared in front of me. "Fix my lunch, quickly." And she scuttled off to the kitchen. I strolled towards the drawing-room, tapping the wooden cane against the floor as I went. Just as I sat down on one of the luxurious, leather armchairs, the doorbell rang and I heard footsteps echoing in the front hall. "Good afternoon," a loud voice boomed. There were then some words exchanged and my Great Aunt's butler came into the drawing-room. "The insurance man is here to see you, ma'am," he said.

"Send him in!" I said, fluttering my hands around my face. The insurance man entered and started explaining about some complicated business. "Help!" I thought and suddenly I found myself being thrown back to the green grass and bright flowers.

Two items now remained. The diamond necklace caught my eye. I fixed it around my neck and suddenly there were bright lights blazing in front of my face and microphones were pushed to my lips. A bulky man, standing beside me, caught hold of my hand and pushed through the crowd. There, parked in front of me was a long, black, chauffeur-driven limousine. As I stepped in, I saw that there was a huge mirror separating the back seat from the front. I stared at my appearance. I was astounded. It appeared I was a movie star. I was young with a peaches 'n' cream complexion and rosebud lips. My gold hair was perfectly placed around my shoulders and I was clothed in a long, black, sequinned dress.

The bulky man was sitting beside me. "Sorry about that," he said in a husky voice. "That's quite all right, dahling," I replied, in a silky voice, moving my hands about, in gestures, my various rings and bracelets sparkling and glittering.

The man started babbling on, in a very business-like manner and I was beginning to get very bored when the words "five million pounds." caught my attention. "If my headmistress could see me now!" I thought, but, to my disappointment, I was brought back to the forest. I sighed and picked up the last item, my headmistress' mortarboard. As soon as I placed it on my head, I found myself sitting in an office.

My headmistress was not a very pleasant person. She was stout with straw-coloured hair and a lopsided smile which was always taken as a warning. Her long black robes fell around her in folds and her tongue was as sharp as her brown eyes which were sunken into her pale face.

I was now this person. As Pam, the secretary came in with some papers, I crackled, "Thank you," and smiled a sickening, superior smile.

But, as I flicked through the papers, I felt totally inferior. They were of a complicated matter which I did not understand. "Oh, no!" I thought desperately. But, just in time, as Pam came back to collect the documents I was flung back to the forest. Just then, Twilight reappeared. "Enough!" I cried. "I don't mind being me any more!" "Good!" smiled Twilight "Now go home and be contented with who you are." And so I walked from the fresh glade and the forest back to my home.

At the door stood Aunt Marge looking anxious. I did not like seeing the plump, usually jolly woman upset as she had been like a mother to myself and my brother, Sam for three years.

"I'm sorry," I said to her timidly. "That's okay Niamh." she replied. Just then my brother whizzed past, shouting. "Uncle Colm's going to kill you!"

"Oh, shut up!" I yelled.

My father's music

by Alison Carey

St John's National School,
Shannon, Co Clare
Joint Third Prize
1995

He teaches me music
And as I sit with hands pressed to whistle,
I see the glint in his eye,
The prided smile on his face,
And I can tell by these small yet capturing things
He loves me in a very special way.

A fire

by Robert Scott

Rockport Preparatory School,
Holywood, Co Down
Joint Second Prize
1991

CHAPTER 1

"I dare you, I double dare you!" Tom shouted.
"Look, all you have to do is stare into the candle flame and put yourself into a trance, then try to sit up, your spirit will leave the body and you can go anywhere, that is if you're not chicken." With this the boys in dorm started to snigger. I don't like being called chicken, but I hate being laughed at.

"O.K., I'll do it," I hissed. I picked up the candle and lit it. As I stared into the flame I heard a voice ask,

"Has it opened yet?" I presumed the voice to be Rory's. Rory isn't the brightest of boys, last week he asked Mrs Pallin when next year was!

'I wonder how I get back into my body?' I was pondering on this thought when suddenly it happened, I began to feel myself being slowly pulled upwards. As I looked back I saw my own lifeless body sitting there.

As I stared I saw the candle drop out of what would be my hand. The pillow caught fire instantly. The fire spread round the dorm and the fire alarm went off. Everyone was in panic but within thirty seconds all the boys were down the fire escape.
Suddenly I remembered something: as I looked around I saw my body, or what was left of it, burnt to cinders.

"Of course," I thought, "Without any spirit to control it, the body couldn't move away from the fire.

"Oh fine," I said to myself, "stuck on earth without a body!"

CHAPTER 2

The sun hung in the sky like a great golden disk, and the sea sparkled. It was the first day of summer, two weeks from the time I had been separated from my body. I had become used to the fact I am not solid matter and therefore can walk through walls and doors. The problem comes when I want to pick something up, my hands just glide through it. I have also found that I don't have to breathe, so I can stay underwater for as long as I want.

Tomorrow all the staff will come back to school, and the children the day after. The school has been done up after the fire. My funeral is next week, although I'm not sure whether to go or not.

I think the only thing that can see or hear me are the rats in the stream, they seem to understand me, but rats are not the best of things to have a conversation with. It is getting lighter at nights now but that doesn't help as I don't have to sleep. It has been like this every day for the last couple of weeks. Hopefully I'll feel better when the teachers come back tomorrow. Funny though, I never thought I'd be happy to see a teacher.

I · CAN · STAY · UNDERWATER
FOR · AS · LONG · AS · I · WANT

CHAPTER 3

The teachers came back today but I still don't feel any better. I found something else out, I can hear what someone is thinking just by looking at them. Mr McManus keeps worrying if he's just a figment of someone else's imagination, although he won't tell anyone about it.

It is night time now and I am going to try to sleep. Tomorrow the pupils come back. I wonder if I grow old in this spirit form?

I woke up with a start.

"I don't believe it," I said to myself, "I slept." Then I noticed something, everything had changed.

"Oh God," I thought. I ran down the stairs into the main hall. I nearly fainted as I saw the date, 11th February, 1994. Suddenly I realised I had been asleep for four years. I walked through the wall and back up to the dorms. As I walked into the dorm I heard rushing water. I ran into the bedroom and saw a body on the floor. Water was gushing over the sides of the bath. The child was obviously dead. Then I remembered something. I had come out of a body so why couldn't I get back into one.

I slowly sank into the lifeless body, it felt weird, my head tingled and I passed out.

When I awoke I was lying on a hospital bed, a nurse was looking at me.

"Where am I?" I asked.

"You nearly drowned, if it wasn't for your matron you'd be dead, you owe her a lot of thanks." she answered. I looked across the room into a mirror, the face was strange, but then I remembered it. It was the boy who had drowned. I let out a sigh of relief.

Back at school one of the masters told me that I reminded him of a boy who died in a fire a few years ago.

"If only he knew," I whispered wryly. "If only he knew."

Pathway to another country - dying the easy way

by David Martin

Headford National School,
Kells, Co Meath
Third Prize
1991

I had one move to checkmate and the chess cup was mine. I moved my rook to the eighth square of the king's file and whispered in a quiet but firm way,
"Mate", and left the room.

That night I could think of nothing but chess and chess pieces. I woke up early that morning because of a strange force which was pulling me away from my bed. I was slowly being dragged towards the window which was fully open. I grabbed onto the window in the hope that I might be able to clamber back inside, but to no avail, for this strange force had me floating in thin air. I was frustrated and frightened.

The next thing I knew was that I was lying next to a large rotten trunk on a bright summer's morning. I rubbed my eyes and stood up. I looked around. But I didn't know this place. It was black and white, everything was chequered. I walked on and there before me was a large board. This board had sixty-four black and white squares. Each square was about two metres wide. I walked on and noticed a small crowd beside the board, but these things were not people, they were all chess pieces, living and man-sized. I rubbed my eyes in the hope that all this might be a dream, but to my dismay this was no dream.

These people then walked onto the board and lined themselves up as though on the coffee table in my own sitting room. I was frightened but in a way I was interested.

By this time the white king was already discussing with his queen what his first move should be. They finally decided to move the pawn in front of the queen forward two places. These moves went on for hours until eventually I noticed a large grin creep across the white king's face as he ordered his rook to move four places forward and while this was happening he shouted in a gleeful manner,

"Mate!"

"It's not," roared the black king.

"No, it's not mate. I'm winning!"

The two white rooks eventually had to carry the heartbroken black king off the board and onto the throne which he had arrived in. By this time the white army were already celebrating and the white king was even drunk. The pawns were celebrating with enormous quantities of chips and sausages and they were mocking the black king who could still be heard crying in the distance.

Suddenly the white queen spotted me and shrieked,

"Capture that thing!"

The whole assembly started to run after me. The knights mounted their horses and began to pick up speed. All the pawns were screaming. I turned and ran knowing I had not a chance of escaping.

"He's mine!" squealed the king's pawn.

"No, he is not, he's mine!" answered the king's knight.

I ran as fast as I could but I couldn't escape the hands of the queen's pawn. I struggled but I was pinned firmly to the ground and therefore was unable to move.

"I've got him!" shouted the queen's pawn, "and did you see the way I closed in on him and it was all my own work and . . . "

"Quiet", rumbled the king in a deep voice, "bring it here to me at once".

The chuffed pawn was happy to drag me towards the king. He dumped me at the king's feet with an enormous smile across his face.

"Huh," said the king, "what is this creature? I have never seen its like before."

"I wouldn't know that sort of thing, what I mean is, I'm only a little pawn."

The Bishops began to laugh.

"Oh, do shut up" muttered the king and the smile quickly left the pawn's face.

They stood me up against a tree and asked me what my name was.

"David" I answered in a quiet tone.

"David?" The king looked puzzled. "What sort of a name is that? Are you a newly developed piece? Try this for size," he said, turning to the queen "pawn to 'King's David's Four'".

THE·CHUFFED·PAWN·WAS·HAPPY·TO·DRAG·ME·TOWARDS·THE·KING·

The whole assembly broke into fits of laughter.

"We must behead him, he's a spy for the black king."
There was a silence.

"Wait a second, I am not a spy," I said hoping to save myself.

"Shut up!" he answered. Then he ordered the king's rook's pawn to fetch the 'headclipper'. I began to panic, but there was nothing I could do. I went through every prayer I knew, repeating them silently to myself but none of them helped me in any way. When the pawn returned with the 'headclipper', I knew I was gone.

Clunk . . .

11 Plus nerves

by Louise Beck

Mill Strand Integrated Primary School,
Portrush, Co Derry/Londonderry
Joint Third Prize
1995

My nerves burst,
They scatter all around my body,
My hands can't keep still,
10 minutes to the death test.
I feel as if my life depends on this test.
All I can think of is Maths, English and Science.
My thoughts swirl around in my head.
My feet start to tap on the ground.
5 minutes to the death test.
My stomach starts to get sore and I feel rather hot.
I read over the rules and then look at my watch.
2 minutes to the death test.
The lady at the top of the room gives out the tests.
10 seconds to the death test.
Everything goes silent and then we begin.
1 hour later it's all over and my nerves disappear.

Christopher's discovery

by Kelly Burnett

Hardy Memorial Primary School,
Richhill, Co Armagh
Second Prize
1992

"Oh, how I wish," said Christopher one day, "that there were still some places in the world to discover."

"Well, there is outer space, you know," his mother said.

And just as he was deciding to be an outer space explorer when he grew up, she added, "I'm going to start cleaning the attic today. That's sort of exploring. Want to come?"

"Yes," said Christopher, taking the brushes and dusters his mother held out. And upstairs they both went. The attic did look mysterious, with dust and cobwebs everywhere. When most of that was cleared away, Christopher and his mother began opening the boxes and trunks.

They found looking over the woollens, that he had outgrown all his winter things, and would need new ones. Christopher liked discovering that he had grown so much. He liked it, too, when his mother opened an old trunk, and brought out pictures of his great-grandparents, and his great-great grand parents. It made him feel important – as if he'd been coming for an awful lot of years.

"Almost since Christopher Columbus discovered America," he told himself.

And then Christopher made a most wonderful discovery.

Up on a shelf was a large box wrapped in old newspaper. Christopher had wondered about it when they were dusting. Now he wondered again, so he took it down.

He carefully unwrapped the paper.

And he opened the lid, and looked inside.

Inside, with tissue paper all around, was the most beautiful model ship he had ever seen. It was painted a dull red, and touched with gold. It had many tiny sails, and on the bow was lettered Santa Maria!

"Columbus's ship!" Christopher cried. "Where did it come from?"

"Oh," said mother, turning around, "It must have come with Grandmother Gilbert's things. Her father was a sea captain, and good at ship models."

Then mother said, "This one's so beautiful that it should be downstairs where we can all enjoy looking at it."

Christopher said, "Could it be in my room?"

"Why, yes," said mother. "Yes, I think it should, after all, it was your discovery, Chris."

So down the stairs went Christopher, to put the Santa Maria on top of the cupboard in his room. And there it stands, to this very day. Except on one day of each year.

Then it sails in the centre of the diningroom table – on a mirror like a calm sea – in honour of Christopher Columbus, and his discovery. And in honour of young Chris, and his discovery, too.

My best day

by Adam Mackin

Kilbroney Primary School,
Rostrevor, Co Down
First Prize
1995

I really like going to my uncle's farm and helping out. My best day was when I was four or five, I saw a cow having a calf for the first time in my life. It was a miracle. However the cow had a problem getting the calf out, so my uncle got my Dad out to the barn. The barn is very smelly and the floor is covered in straw and cow dung. Dad told Jo and I to get the Jack. A Jack is a machine which works like a lever. You tie a rope around the calf's legs and push the lever down, as you do the rope tightens and pulls the calf out.

The next time I will know how to deliver a calf but, when Dad and Paddy did it, the cow fainted. Dad and Paddy were in a panic. They were hitting the cow's bum trying to wake it up, and it did finally wake up.

After a very hard effort they delivered the calf. The calf was a friesian bullock the same as its mum and dad. Uncle Paddy was very pleased with the friesian bullock.

My first night without the light on

by Daniel Boyle

Chapel Road Primary School,
Derry/Londonderry
Joint Second Prize
1991

One evening my parents said, "Since you are getting to be a big boy, we have decided that it is time for you to go to sleep without the light on!" I was horrified! What, no light at night? Really, my parents were asking far too much of me! I continued with more thoughts. My parents love me, don't they? Then why make me turn off the light when I don't want to? These questions crossed my mind. Then I decided they were just being mean.

That night, my parents turned out the light. I couldn't see much in the dark. It was very strange. I was scared. Horrible thoughts came into my head. At every horrible thought I gave a gulp! My brother from across the room said, "Will you stop that gulping and go to sleep?" A long half hour later I heard my brother snoring. I began to feel really sorry for myself. The sorrier I got the sadder I felt.

When I was almost crying something caught my eye through the curtains. I sat up, then I got out of bed and walked over to the window. I drew aside the curtains. The sky was full of stars. Some of them were really beautiful. I could see many stars twinkling in the sky. I thought to myself, "They really are beautiful, no mistake about it." Then I thought I saw a red star! Whatever can it be? I looked and looked. I could see a couple of constellations whose names I knew.

These were Orion's Belt and the Plough. I knew I should be in bed but I couldn't tear myself away from that window.

I dragged a chair up to the window and sat there for some time. I began to feel tired so I went back to bed. I slept for about an hour and then I woke up. I lay there thinking about the stars. When I could stand it no longer I went back to the window. I sat down in the chair and looked out again. The stars seemed even brighter! I marvelled at them. Then I saw the moon – it was a full moon that night and it was almost dazzling to look at it. After a while I fell asleep by the window. I dreamt that I was flying towards the stars and that I picked them up one by one. Then I threw them across the sky.

I woke up. "Phew! Some dream," I thought. I gazed at the stars a little longer. I couldn't resist saying, "Twinkle, Twinkle, Little Star." I felt very happy. I even winked at a star. I just felt good. Suddenly a strange pink glow appeared across the sky. The stars went out, one by one. I felt scared. What was happening? Then I knew. It was dawn. I suddenly felt very tired. I dragged myself over to my bed. Just as I touched the pillow with my head I fell fast asleep.

It was morning. My mummy had a hard job waking me up. I gave a yawn. "Oh, mum, do I have to get up?" I said.

"Yes, you have to go to school. Now come along," mummy said. I dragged myself up to the kitchen. I sat down and cheered up when I saw my favourite breakfast on the table. It was a soft boiled egg and soldiers. I told my parents about last night.

"No wonder you're tired," said mummy.

"Hmm," said daddy. "I know where there is an Astronomy club. Would you like to join it?"

"Yes, please," I said delighted.

"Gracious," said mummy, "you'll be late for school!"

I groaned, "Do you have to mention school at the breakfast table?" Everyone burst out laughing.

Winter's wrath

by Anna Murray

Darragh Cross Primary School,
Saintfield, Co Down
Second Prize
1993

The sky darkens
Clouds call forth their families
Casting dark shadows around
Mean and evil they spread
Their shrouds
An ominous sign!
Droplets of rain, tiny at first
Tap our heads and window panes.
Slowly, slowly puddles shape
Then a deluge
Sweeps across our towns and lands
Helped by an angry wind
At first a whisper, then a roar
What will quench his craving thirst?

In the woodlands, trees succumb
Breaking branches, hopes are dashed
As giant trees by roots are slashed
Years of effort strewn about.
In the towns, an eerie sound
        Doors slam
        Gates crash
        Boxes roll
        Bins topple
        Bottles smash
What an anger winter's unleashed.

Up and down the streets
Leaves and rubbish zip along
Dancing amidst this angry throng.
Alone, a cyclist fighting back
Holding hard against attack
Footsteps trudge close to walls
Brollies, hats fight off the squall
As the storm hunts its prey.
Mercilessly it reaches out
Its shrieking fangs
To grab and crush
All in its way.

Birds fly low to their homes
To find shelter from this foe
Animals cower in their shed
Not too sure what it is they dread
Buildings standing, start to sway
Soon demolished on the way
Out at sea, boats rock and roll
Foam spits and frolics against the bay
Throughout the night storms
Echo and growl
An angry lion on its prowl
At first light silence abounds
Birds were all that made their sounds
What damage lay for us today?
"Storms Lashed"
The papers say.

Runaway girl

by Charmaine McNally

Chapel Road Primary School,
Derry/Londonderry
Highly Commended
1992

"You make me sick the lot of you", said Catherine.

"It's all right, calm down" said her mother trying to comfort her.

"You're the only one who cares anymore".

Catherine was having great problems at school and at home. Her father did something to upset her every day. Catherine was a sensible child who took everything to heart. She told her mammy she couldn't take anymore and was leaving.

"Don't go, I'll patch things up, I promise".

Catherine heard the same old story every time. No-one really knew what Catherine's father was like. Catherine thought it was like living in hell with him.

That night everything stood still and quiet, Catherine took a last look at her prison. The tears dropped from her rosy cheeks. She didn't know whether she felt sorrow or joy. Maybe she felt a bit of both. Her mammy thought if she ever did go she would grow up too quickly and have to take on big responsibilities that she could not cope with.

It was difficult for Catherine. She always said she would leave but Catherine could never face up to it.

When everyone was about to go to work and school, Catherine's mother was very worried and went into her room to check on her. "Oh God, I knew this would happen". There was a note on Catherine's bed. Her mammy read it aloud so there would be no mistake. It read in the neat hand-writing of Catherine. "You're the only one I love, mammy, remember that. I can't stand living here anymore. I know you said you would patch everything up, but I know what father is like. I'll try to phone you. Sorry. Catherine".

Catherine's mammy lay on the bed holding a picture of her. The only sound that could be heard was the soft weeping of the mother. Meanwhile, Catherine was on the back of a bus thinking about what she had done. It was confusing for her. Had this fourteen year-old girl done the right thing? Maybe. Maybe not. "Where am I going to stay?" thought Catherine. It was winter. She couldn't sleep on the streets.

When Catherine finally came to a town she knew nothing about, she took one look around and saw that the market place was crowded with girls and boys her own age. They sat in tiny groups talking to each other. They didn't seem worried at all. Did Catherine know what she was in for? No. She walked around the market place to see if anyone would take any notice.

As the day moved on, Catherine had met two friends – Peter, sixteen, who had run away from home when he was fourteen because he was being abused. The other person was Laura who was fourteen too. She ran away because of the same problem as Catherine. Peter was like a big brother to her. He looked after her and cared for her. Catherine was a little abashed when the other youths talked to her about things she didn't know. When Catherine told her two new friends she had nowhere to stay, they offered her a place to stay.

"It might not be like your real home, but at least you'll be warm", said Peter, thinking she would refuse because of the way he had put it. But Catherine didn't care what she slept in, as long as she didn't freeze to death. That night, when Catherine caught the first look at her room, she shuddered. She had a cardboard box flattened with a thin blanket. There was nothing else in the room. Catherine thought the house might have been a bit furnished, but it wasn't. She listened to the others talking, but it wasn't very interesting, so she stopped. She felt uncomfortable and sick. The floor was carpeted with thick dust that made her sneeze, and the damp made her cough.

Catherine thought only about the good times at home. "Maybe I should have just moved out and stayed at my brother's home". Now this girl was really confused, maybe she did love her father deep down. Catherine was having second thoughts. Thinking about her parents made her sob. It was only when Catherine started to listen to her friends talking again that she found out they were squatting. Her mind was like a crossroads. Eventually, she fell asleep and when she woke she found that the house was empty. The place was empty. The only thing that was found was a letter that said "Thanks for the twenty pounds and the savings book." "They were supposed to be my friends", thought Catherine.

Now Catherine hadn't got any money to buy food or pay for B & B. Catherine pushed herself to the ground, slowly put her hands over her face and cried. She cried for hours until she heard voices of people talking about a runaway girl. Catherine scrambled out the back door. Posters of a runaway girl were in all shop windows. Catherine took a glance at one. It was her! There was a reward for anyone who could bring her home. Now Catherine couldn't walk in the streets without anyone recognising her. All day long, Catherine sat at the back of a park thinking. In just one day, Catherine was used to being homeless. She didn't cry anymore. She didn't feel sorry for herself or her father. Catherine wasn't worried about what people would say back home. Catherine was really sick. She needed a doctor, but she couldn't have a doctor. He or she would take her back home.

Catherine wandered round the dark streets, cold and sick. It was safe. Catherine stopped to watch some television in a shop window. The news came on. "What is this, Save Catherine Week?", said Catherine as the news was mainly about her. She ran to the nearest phone box and reversed the charges. It was her mother who had answered. "I'm not coming home", said Catherine, "I can't. I love you". That was the last words before Catherine put the phone down. "Ouch", cried Catherine as someone grabbed her shoulder. It was a policeman. Catherine didn't argue with him because she knew policemen were powerful.

"You're the young lady on the telly, aren't you?", he said in a husky voice. Catherine nodded her head slowly. The hand on Catherine's shoulder felt heavy and hard. He held Catherine by the shoulder until he got her into the police car. There was a police-woman there too. Catherine sat in the car patiently, saying nothing to anyone. Catherine started to look out the window. She recognised the highway. This was the one she travelled on when she was on the bus. Catherine started to sweat. Her coughing and sneezing got worse.

"You need to see a doctor", said the police-woman. "You're very ill".

No-one had noticed that Catherine was panicking. She knew her father was going to do something to her when she got home. Panicking made Catherine sleepy. She went out like a light. The next thing Catherine knew she was in her own bed.

By her bed sat a middle-aged woman. It was a doctor. The doctor told her not to get out of bed. Catherine wasn't even listening to her. Catherine didn't eat nor speak to anyone for two days. Every time someone tried to talk to her she turned her head.

"What you did was stupid", said everyone, even her friends.

Every time her father was in the house, she went out. Catherine never really spoke to her parents until the day she got her own flat. Then everything changed. Catherine could talk to her parents about anything.

My gran

by Amanda Hamilton

Glebe National School,
Donegal Town
Third Prize
1992

My Gran is Sunday surprises and apple pie. Her wrinkles are like the rippling sand on a golden beach, behind shiny spectacles are her soft hazelnut eyes. Sometimes I touch her hands, the backs of them feel as soft as her woollen cardigan but the palms are rough from working.

When Gran cooks she wears a daisy patterned apron – when she makes scones it becomes dusted with flour – she smells of baking and rosewater.

On cold winter nights she sits beside a blazing fire flicking through her photo album and recalls happy memories of her childhood. In spring and summer you will find her in the garden with her plants and flowers, her hands and fingernails covered with soil. My Gran walks slowly because of her ageing bones. Seeing her grandchildren makes her very happy, and I love my Gran very much.

Old

by Maeve Lewis

Hazelwood Integrated Primary School,
Newtownabbey, Co Antrim
Second Prize
1994

The old woman sat asleep in her chair,
Rocking to and fro,
She had a range of wonderful tales,
She knew all there was to know.

She told the children tales of her youth,
When she was young and fit,
And of how she played outside all day
And never stopped to sit.

Now she had grown old,
Wrinkly and grey
Her blue hands knitted
Night and day.

Her frizzy grey hair
Was always a mess
And she always wore
The same flowered dress.

But the old woman still
Sat asleep in her chair
Rocking to and fro
And she still had a range of wonderful tales
And knew all there was to know.

Old house

by Alexandra Faldina

English Specialised School No 455
St Petersburg
2nd Prize Winner
1996

This story was written in English.
The editor has not made any changes to the text.

Time flies and it is impossible to stop it, to wreck it, to make an hour from a second. There is no handyman which could do this. With the time everything changes, everything gets old and becomes poor and needless. Everyone is to put up with that, but how hard it is sometimes to part with a dear toy with which I have played, ever after I remember myself, slept clasping her and cuddling to myself nearby. How hard it is to depart from a native house to another one.

Every summer we go to the village. There, near the forest, house is standing, in which we live by a big family, with great-grandpa and great-grandma, going away in winter and leaving them together – an old house and old people.

But with the time it had became so old, that it was dangerous to stay there. The house had nodded awry and disrepaired. We saw that and began to build a new house and at last summer it was ready.

A new, big house. That's wonderful. And, of course, we reheated (had a house-warming) on that day, when the last works were ended. We were busy all that day. The neighbourhood came for us to look at it, to admire it and to outspeak their opinions. In the evening the background became more calm.

It was late. I went to bed. It was very cosy at home, but outdoors it was windy. All heaped warmth emanated from the furnace. The wind gradually lulled. I couldn't sleep. It was already not warm, but hot and cold at the same time. There was one feeling in myself, but I didn't know what it was. It enlarged in this silence, which folded me. I understood! I pitied that house, old house, derelict house. In that time it was alone. There was no person, which he could warm, mantle across his doors. But ones it building, everyone wanted him. That was long ago. A lot of people, a lot of generations had been living there. Much of things he had seen on his century. The house had lived through the wars together with people, with people had grieved, had chuckled and all the time he had helped them. A lot of things he had known, had heard. And no one will know about this. He keeps this only inside himself and he doesn't say this to anyone, because, perhaps, can't talk or maybe no one has asked him and didn't think about this. House – it is a history. And if someone asks him, maybe, he will narrate everything that he has been keeping in himself for a long time, but, maybe will not recite and will keep all in him forever to the end of his days. Nature has a lot of mysteries. People can't say, I think, that the house can't have a soul or some other feelings, but if it is really so, I think, there can be some exceptions.

Perhaps, house is living by our memory... How can we forget that minutes of happiness, which we had there? We can take, for example, an old furnace. Furnace! In the cold evenings, lying on the furnace, our grandpa recited us different fairy tales, falling asleep on the most interesting places. We awaked him, but he couldn't remember on which place he had stopped and so he began from the beginning... and who didn't listen to the songs of a cold wind in the chimney.

And samovar! I remember the bluster of water infusing in to the samovar, the boom of the flame. Through some minutes all this brassy motion began to brawl, like a flat summer rain. I remember that little swelter from the burning carbon, little clank, that comes in to any bellicose pipe, hot, shining sides of the samovar, in which it was possible to look. And how it seems to me, the house looked at them with great pleasure, glancing by his windows and chuckling that all the people are gathering together again over to tea.

In autumn there was a beautiful smell of dry apples and mushrooms.

This house never been congested. I remember that hilarious comings of the guests from all the world. There was enough place, warmth and cosiness for everyone.

I don't want to talk about the house in the past tense. The house is like a man – time comes and he becomes old and needless. It is cold inside the house and rueful. He understood that he had been left not for a winter but forever. Time comes and the house must only wait for his last days recalling all that, what had happened in him all these long years.

Here my dreams little by little began to disappear, and I fell asleep. In the morning I parted my alarms with my parents. And we decided: the old house would live. We would do over him, and he would afresh make people happy, warm them and talk stories about himself and about people, which lived in him.

Poems

by Gavin Daly

St Killian's National School
Crossreagh, Co Cavan
Highly Commended
1996

Quern stone

Sweat flowed down my red cheeks
I was slowly grinding
The dry ripe wheat with the
Round rough solid stone.
Slowly and endlessly the white
Powdery lumps appeared between the stones.
We collect the precious wheat carefully
Licking our lips and dreaming.

Avril

I came home from school on that
Warm summer's day.
I walked down the rough stony lane.
My father stood outside peering helplessly
At the window.
My mother ran out the brown door.
Tears ran down her pale cheeks as
She walked me to our neighbours' house.
Neil and Eimear were there
Confused like me.
We played quietly with Lego.
That evening we were left home.
Relations and friends were there sitting around
The blazing fire talking quietly to each other.
They sipped cups of tea all saying how sorry they were.
But there was no cuddly baby in the cot.

Starry night sky

The snow is falling on that
Thick bare oak tree.
Peaceful candles are on
Every window.
Lights are flashing on the
Colourful Christmas tree.
The figures in the crib are still
Like the cold snowy night.

Aunties, uncles and cousins
come in all dressed up smart.
All of them eating away at mum's
Best Christmas pudding.
The children are all excited
Telling each other
What they are getting from Santy
As they pull the Christmas crackers.
The adults are sitting around the blazing fire
Gossiping to each other.

And when they leave
I look up into the starry night sky.

My mysterious corner

by Sergei Avdeyev

Economic Secondary School No 166
St Petersburg
3rd Prize Winner
1996
This story was written in English.
The editor has not made any changes to the text.

Near the village where I usually spend my summer holidays there is a small place which is dear and sweet to me. A small forest lake is situated there. Everybody admires the lake with its clear water and its sandy beaches and soft green grass. This place is so beautiful that it touches the heart of everyone who has a happy chance to be nearby.

I saw this lake for the first time when my father and I went on a hike one day. I didn't expect that it would be so interesting.

And here I am, standing on its bank and all wrapped up in my deep thoughts. A lot of pretty birds are singing their wonderful songs high up in the air and on the trees. The lake seems to invite me to bathe and swim in its pure blue warm waters. I can't help myself jumping into the lake and the next moment I am swimming slowly on my back admiring the blue cloudless skies.

Suddenly some strange sound interrupts my thoughts in the water. It is a splash of an unknown fish who is the master of this lake. The lake seems to me to be its own palace. I ought to remember that I am only her guest. To my mind she wants to amuse me and to play a joke on me at the same time. My visit to her palace was exciting. I am leaving her palace fresh and full of power. I really enjoyed her beautiful manners and graceful dances around me.

Now I'm lying quietly on the golden sandy beach and having a rest.

But my fairy–tale has no end. Just some distance off I notice a strange red eye watching me carefully. It's a strawberry who is inviting me to eat it. I take it tenderly in my hands and can't tear my eyes off it. So beautiful and sweet it looks to me. When I put it into my mouth I feel how tasty it is. It simply melts in my mouth.

To be honest I haven't seen yet anything more beautiful than that mysterious corner with its wonderful inhabitants.

My secret place –

The gloomy cave

by Ryan Green
Harberton Special School, Belfast
3rd Prize
1996

"Can you keep a secret? I have a very special place and I am going to take you there as long as you will tell no-one! Right! Come with me! Stop dragging along! It gets misty on the way so watch out for rocks! We just have to pass the old leafy oak tree. Here is the tree. Now you have to swing on this rope to get across. No don't go that way, that's the traps. So swing! That's good. Here I come. Look out! Walk on! Here it is, this cave. Come in and I'll show you around. It gets dark and gloomy, as you see, and it is big. There is a special room. That's where I keep all my special things. There it is, very gloomy in all other parts of the cave. That is why you need a lantern. Now the traps. This is my best trap. See that. The spiky acorns fall down and hit you on the head. This is the ditch you have to swing over. See! It is camouflaged so that you will fall down into it. You should come down sometime. Do you hear that? That tells you that the red moon is out tonight. That means it is a special night. I'm going to have to go now. See you tomorrow. Do not tell anyone! Right! See you."

The loft
by Gillian Simpson

Harberton Special School, Belfast
4th Prize
1996

Three or four years ago my Dad converted the loft into a room. There is a middle bit and quite a small bottom bit. Where the boiler is my Dad blocked it off so there was a little space. On the other side there is a window where the sun comes in. I hung a pink blanket over it. I go up when I am sad and scared. I have two of my favourite bears up too. When I go up I get so comfortable I sometimes fall asleep. Once or twice I have fallen asleep all night and all day. I play with my cats up there too. I love to go up to my secret place.

Under the stairs
by Jordan Stewart

Harberton Special School, Belfast
Highly Commended
1996

My secret place is under the stairs. It is a cupboard. It is small and dark and cramped because there is a lot of junk. I can just get in but my brother can't. I go there when I don't want to do things for my mum or dad so I wait there until my mum or dad calls for my brother or sister. I just sit and sit until I don't have to do anything. Sometimes I have sat so long that I have fallen asleep. There are a lot of books and a bag of tools and boxes. When my mum buys a new carpet and there is any left over I will take it and put it in my secret place so I will have something to sit on. In my secret place I can keep things from my brother and sister, like sweets and books. I put football posters up in it. But when I get older it will be used for junk again. When I am older I will not have use for it any more so I don't want to grow up!

Poems

by Sarah Boucher

Dalkey School Project National School, Co Dublin
4th Prize
1996

What is peace?

Rosscarberry last summer
In afternoon heat
Cantering on Spirit
The breeze in his name
The breeze in my face
His hooves beat the peace

Temptation

Glazed at the top
The lovely sweet icing
Swirled pastry like a twisted snake teases you
Makes your mouth water.
The chewy sweet raisins
Encased in the glistening icing
White sticky covers your fingertips
Messes the couch
It's all over your mouth
When it's all gone
You wish for some more
Do you think you were wrong
To just gobble it down?

What is peace?

by Fionn Toland

Scoil Cholmcille, Letterkenny
Co Donegal
3rd Prize
1996

Carl slipped the pen knife into his pocket and felt around a bit more. But there was nothing. He pulled his two bony hands out of the hole and sighed. Carl lived in Belfast near the city centre and this was the only chance he got to get away from it all. He knew it was only a murky swamp littered with anything you could imagine, but he liked it.

He was tall for his age, dark-haired and his blue eyes always seemed to glisten. He had blue jeans that hugged his long stretched legs. The pocket was half ripped and he always wondered how anything managed to stay in it. He wore an old green sweater that was ripped where it overlapped his jeans and a baseball cap which had the name of some basketball team which he had never heard of. His runners were the only half decent things he wore.

He was searching in a small hole where he had seen teenagers drinking and had found a pocket knife. He saw some soldiers and started making faces at them. They always seemed to be looking at him. But he knew it was going to be like that since the cease-fire had ended, always having to go in early, always having to take extra

HE • DARTED • ACROSS • THE • MARSHLAND

care. Soldiers – they were the worst, always looking, always asking questions. They were in combat gear with ankle high boots, their grim faces smeared with camouflage and hate written all over them.

He darted across the marshland, jumping over rocks. He stopped and thought. Why not run away? Say, just for a day or two, or maybe a week, or why not a month? He could really get away then. Why not? This question kept rolling over in his head. Imagine, no early nights, no questions, no beady eyes piercing you with their look!

He peered at the forest in the distance and suddenly started sprinting over to it. He jumped the neat, well- made fence with the smooth posts. He slid down a ramp and down to a small peaceful stream. The fumes of Belfast, the talk, the commotion, the confusion was all leaving him now. In a few hours his parents would have a small search party after him, secretly relieved he was gone. But he didn't care. He was free and he could do what he wanted.

It was getting very dark so he slipped into a crevice. It was surrounded with trees and the gentle sway of them lulled him to sleep. The next day he awoke to shouts and cries of children, soldiers, parents and the barking of dogs. He bolted down an embankment, over a fence and into a field. It seemed to stretch for miles but he reached the other side before anyone came into view. They were searching for him. They actually cared! He kept running and running jumped into a fast flowing river and waded over to the other side. He grabbed a tree, but slipped. He was swept down the river. He was going to die! But suddenly he felt two hands grasp his waist. He was pulled out on to the bank. When he opened his eyes a soldier was looking down at him. But the eyes, in the serious weatherbeaten face, were kind. "Carl", he said, "you were lucky".

What my senses experienced

by Mairead Smyth

St Killian's National School,
Crossreagh, Co Cavan
1st Prize
1996

Walking, hearing the brisk leaves beneath my feet,
The stillness of the whitewashed countryside.
Looking down to see each blade of grass
Coated in a magical white.
I feel the sensation of cold air
Whipping my face numb.

I ran from the school
But not quickly enough
For the sunmelt had come
And all that was left was
The usual green
Like nothing had happened.

Wind

by Maria Coyne

Scoil Mhuire na gCnoc,
Knock, Co Mayo
Highly Commended
1996

I hurried home from school one day
The wind blew strong and hard
It crouched behind each corner
Dragging rubbish round the yard.

It tattered the clothes on the line
It whistled through the trees
Leaves fluttered wildly
As it scattered them on the street.

It gusted the dust along the road
And rolled across the fields
It whirled and swirled around my feet
My balance was hard to keep.

Puffing and panting I reached the gate
The wind slammed it shut with a crash
It whistled in as I opened the door
And it came to rest on the mat.

Kissing in the street

by Daniel Devlin

Windmill Integrated Primary School
Dungannon, Co Tyrone
Highly Commended
1996

One day I was walking down the street with my pocket money, when suddenly my mum comes along and says, "Daniel, have you spent any of your pocket money yet?" "No," I said. "Well, here's an extra pound." She gave me a kiss and said, "Look after yourself," and she walked on. Oh boy! Was I embarrassed or was it just my imagination, I FELT I WAS GOING PURPLE!

Well, I walked on and along comes my granny, and she said "Hello, Sweety, I was talking to your mum up the road there." "I... I... I..." and before I could say what I was going to say, down came two big wrinkly lips onto my cheek, and then she walked on. "Good," I said, "I'm glad no one saw that." I stood still for a second, then walked on.

For about twenty minutes I was lonely, until along comes my girlfriend and asks "Would you like to go to the cinema to watch Father of Bride Part II?" "Of course. I'll pay you in." "No, you've been paying me in for the last three months, it's about time I paid myself in." "Well, fair's fair." "But I prefer it if I paid you in." "It's alright," she said, "Look, we'd better hurry. It starts in five minutes." So we sat where we could get a good view of the screen and watched the movie.

When it was over, she said "I'm walking home, would you like to come with me?" I said, "Would you like a burger first...I'll pay." "No thanks," she said "I have to get home for eight o'clock. . .Come on, it's getting dark." "All right, but I did offer."

Later about ten past eight we were at the bottom of the street. My girlfriend said, "Thanks for walking me home," and gave me a kiss on the lips and went into her house.

I walked along the street and into my house, dived onto my bed and said to myself, "What a day I've had. . .what a day!"

My funny friend

by Maria McGurk

Scoil Aodha Rua agus Nuala
Co Donegal
Highly Commended 1996

Saturday morning
Oh! What a thrill.
I've just met my
New friend Bill.

He just appeared
Out of nowhere.
He has a plummy round nose
And slimy green hair.

His feet are HUGE
His runners: dirty, red.
His knees are knobbly,
Slender is his head.

His ears are fantastic,
Full of stubbly hair.
His lips are bananas.
Eat them if you dare.

On that Monday
Getting ready for work.
Bill jabbed Dad in the
Ankle with a fork.

Tuesday was a sad day.
Mummy sat on Bill.
I know she didn't see him
But he went to hospit–ill.

Wednesday was a funny day
There was a drastic mess.
We made a brilliant camping tent
Out of Mummy's Sunday dress.

Shopping day was Thursday.
We nimbly stole the sweets
Off the sweetie counter.
It wasn't much of a feast.

Alas, the day was Friday
When glee came to an end.
Dad baked Bill in the oven
Farewell, my funny friend.

Let me stay

by Oliver Logan

Royal & Prior Comprehensive School
Raphoe, Co Donegal
Highly Commended
1996

10.00 P.M. Please let me stay
Just 'til this game is won
Don't send me to bed
While I'm having such fun.

It's comfortable here
There's a great show on TV
My eyes are wide open
Look, can't you see?

I'm happy here
So just for today
Don't send me to bed
Let me stay, let me stay.

8.00 A.M. Please let me stay
The night's gone so fast
Don't make me get up
'til my dream has passed.

It's comfortable here
and I'm not yet awake
Just five more minutes
Oh! My poor head does ache.

I'm happy here
Can't I sleep in today?
Don't make me get up
Let me stay, let me stay.

Silence

by Alan Laird

Convoy Joint National School,
Co Donegal
Highly Commended
1996

The coils of rope are hanging against the harbour wall. The lobster pots are stacked one by one. The trawlers' engines have stopped working. Shrill shrieking seagulls fly in circles above the harbour, waiting for the engines to start up and the fog of smoke to appear over the sky like a surrounding blanket, but the engines remained silent. The fish merchants are turned back and workers in the fish factory are not at work today. They are paying their respects to Patrick Murphy who died last night trying to earn a living at sea.

Daydreams

by David Bird

Donaghadee Primary School, Co Down
Highly Commended
1996

Mr Banks think I'm listening but NO
I'm caught on the sail of a windmill. . .
Stranded on a distant planet.
Racing motorbikes on a beach. . .
Eating till I bust
Or shooting ducks

Mr Banks thinks I'm Tipp-
Exing my mistakes but No!. . .
I'm painting Van Gogh's
Work of Art
I'm racing Nigel Mansell
Going over a waterfall

Mr Banks thinks I'm
Drinking my Pepsi
But I'm In the pub. . .
Jumping out of an aeroplane,
Cycling down a hill. . .
Climbing up a rock
YIKES! I've
Fallen off the table.

Haircuts

by Stephen Collins

St Columba's College, Stranorlar, Co Donegal
Highly Commended
1996

Harecuts, haircuts, rare cuts, nearcuts,
not cut, somecut, need it cut, no cut,
spike cut, gelcut, well cut, badcut,
soon cut, softcut, hardcut, whencut,
long cut, shortcut, tightcut, loose cut,
fuzzycut, baldycut, shaggycut, strongcut,
straightcut, bentcut, sidecut, all haircuts.
Greasecut, backcut, scarecut, squarecut,
darecut, flarecut, nowcut, thencut,
nearcut, donecut, fatcut, thincut,
downcut, upcut, shavencut, ravencut,
razorcut, scissorcut, shearercut, hedgecut, uppercut,
dogcut, catcut, hedgehogcut, badgercut,
sloppedcut, lotcut, notmuchcut, toomuchcut,
allcut, notallcut, nearallcut, smallcut.
Harecuts, haircuts, rarecuts, nearcut,
notcut, somecut, needitcut, no cut,
spikecut, gelcut, wellcut, badcut,
who gives a heck as long as it's a haircut.

Planks galore

Feidhlim Brogan

Adhamhnáin Naofa National School,
Derrybeg, Co Donegal
Highly Commended
1996

The only time I ever had any interest in planks of wood was when I tried to build a treehouse, which of course I drastically failed. But on the 23rd February 1992 I was amazed at the sight of not a few but hundreds and hundreds of planks floating on the surface of the sea and being washed onto the sandy shores of Gweedore.

On that Saturday morning I remember my father and I were bird-watching. We were looking for the Snowy Owl that my father thought was a figment of my imagination. As the wind gusted straight through my clothes I looked towards the mountains and then in the direction of the deserted islands with my binoculars. I paused for a moment and I heard my father ask, "Can you see it? Give me a look." As I stared in disbelief I could see hundreds of planks, like Viking ships drifting towards the shore. It was like a dream. It was unbelievable. When my father saw me staring so hard he looked out to sea and he asked if I was seeing what he was. I replied slowly as I was just snapping out of my trance, "I think so." When we both recovered from the shock we walked over the soft wet ground towards the beach. Unfortunately the planks were not ashore yet. We headed back home because my father who's a doctor often had many house calls awaiting him, but we decided to come down to the shore later that evening. We innocently supposed that no one would discover our precious floating treasure. As we drove away in the car I looked out the back window longingly at our planks, I couldn't wait to get a hold of them. As I gazed at the floating Armada I could see my treehouse finally taking shape.

NO GROWN UPS NO GIRLS
PRIVITE NO WAY IN

During supper that evening I told my mother what we had discovered. We were really excited. Afterwards we hitched up the trailer and set off in the direction of the beach. As we drove quickly down the pot–holed road, we were surprised and disappointed at what met us at the shore. It was like a sight from Baywatch, people everywhere. As we stood high up on the dunes we watched the incredible sight of people scrambling all over the beach dragging planks and bundling them together. They were so protective, like a dog and its litter. We watched them wade into the freezing sea and being splashed by the waves, to retrieve as many planks as possible. It was such an unbelievable sight.

We sadly made our way down the sandy steep dunes to the beach but it was so packed we could hardly move, let alone drag planks. We managed to retrieve half a dozen planks, but we gave up helplessly. Everybody was practically at each other's throats, even our next door neighbours who were our best friends.

After about an hour we had our planks safely secured on the trailer. They were good big planks which were about twelve feet long and roughly two inches thick, the ends were painted green and they had a stamp faintly printed on them. When we got home we stacked them up cross-ways to let the air circulate through them so they would not rot. My father had already decided what he wanted to build, a kennel for the dogs! As we looked out our kitchen window we could see that the traffic towards the beach was now getting very heavy, there were tractors, trailers, cars, vans, every type of vehicle you could imagine hurrying towards the beach so they could quickly load up and as soon as possible come back for more. Who could ever imagine a traffic jam like that on our once quiet country lane. I knew it would be the talk of the parish for many weeks. I was right because it caused a lot of excitement. That night we watched the line of tractors going up and down the lane and we could see the bright beams lit up on the shore and the rumbling noise of tractors pulling their heavy load. Las Vegas had finally come to the sandy hills of Donegal.

Haiku

by Finn O'Sullivan

Dalkey School Project National School, Co Dublin
2nd Prize
1996

Reflection

A calm pool, crystal
Clear daffodils bowing
and springing away

Snow

Crystalline mantle
Of virgin snow glistening
In the dawn

Shocked numb

by Mairead Smyth
St Killian's National School,
Crossreagh, Co Cavan
1st Prize
1996

Puffins' plumage blends
with the vivid sea-sprayed rocks.
Plunging heads vanish and reappear
like the water had shocked them numb
Emerging with a beakful of
Slender sand eels.

The stone

by Kayleigh Clarke
St John's Primary School, Derry/Londonderry
Highly Commended
1996

Oh! stone, cold from the sea,
Hard like an iron bar but light to lift,
Fossil of millions of years ago.
Now in a plastic container
In a Primary School of the 90's
I wonder where you will end?
Where will you turn up next?
Lost on a beach or in another child's hand
Just like mine?
Or moulded together in a brick
In a building or skyscraper?
Who knows?

Hey! That's cool!

by Laura Gallagher

St Columba's College, Stranorlar, Co Donegal
3rd Prize
1996

Jimmy McCarthy was always regarded as a "different" sort of boy by his neighbours in Towtheline. As a young child he was not interested in playing hurling, a game which was regarded as being almost as important as religion by the rest of the inhabitants of this East Cork Village.

By the time he was eight even his parents were concerned that Jimmy was spending too much time by himself. They would urge him to leave his room, where he spent hours each day reading, and play with the other children. Jimmy hated the silly games that the local children played and especially hated to play with the likes of Ben O'Sullivan.

Ben was the best hurler on the street and, although smaller, he instilled terror in Jimmy by the way he mocked and taunted him in front of the others. Jimmy wasn't a good hurler and this made him the butt of Ben's jokes. Jimmy would be put in goals. Then Ben would show off his skills and score a goal, and as his team mates rushed to congratulate him he would raise his hand in the air and say, "That was cool." Jimmy hated being made look stupid so his appearances on the street with a hurley stick became rarer and rarer.

When he was twelve Jimmy was sent to St Finbarr's Secondary School. To his dismay he ended up in the same class as Ben. Ben soon became popular with his class mates and there was rivalry to be included in his circle of friends. By the age of fourteen Ben was smoking up to ten cigarettes a day. "It's cool to smoke" he told his mates and before long some of them were smoking as well. Ben was always conscious of style and fashion, often trying to wear some of his own more glamourous clothes instead of the school uniform. Once when a teacher asked him why he had shaven off his hair, Ben replied, with a smirk, "I think it's cool."

Jimmy, on the other hand, despite being a very clever student, had few friends at St Finbarr's. As the years went by he seemed to accept that Ben would always be popular and was pleased if he himself escaped with being taunted. Only Maureen Bourke, a girl from near his home village, whom he helped with homework, paid any attention to him, and even she was afraid to be seen to be too friendly, knowing that she would be teased if she appeared to be friends with what Ben O'Sullivan described as "a drip" who went to First Aid class with his sister in preference to going to the under 18's disco with "the lads".

Jimmy got five A's and three B's in his leaving certificate and went to study law in Dublin and, although he came home every second weekend, he had little direct contact with the other youths in Towtheline. He had heard that Ben O'Sullivan was working in his father's garage, but had developed a drink problem and had been in trouble with the guards. But Ben did not worry Jimmy now, as he had plenty of friends in Dublin.

It was during mid-term break in his last year in university that Jimmy was invited to Maureen Bourke's twentyfirst birthday party in her mother's house just outside Towtheline. "It'll be nothing flashy – just a gathering of old friends," she promised.

Jimmy felt completely out of place at Maureen's party. Although he had been made very welcome, he found, as the evening wore on, that he had very little in common with the rest. Their lifestyles were different and he found it difficult to get involved in their conversations. "I hear you're studying law," said Ben O'Sullivan. "That's cool, I must send for you the next time the guards get me," he laughed.

It was about half past ten when Mrs Bourke went to prepare food in the kitchen. She was not long gone when the house shook with a bang and a fireball from an exploded gas cylinder engulfed the house. There was panic as everyone clamoured to get outside.

People shouted and screamed as others pushed and trampled them. When outside, Maureen was hysterically trying to get back in to rescue her mother, but she was held back. "It's too dangerous," she was told. There was a state of complete confusion and terror. Had everyone else got out? Someone shouted: "Where's Jimmy McCarthy? He must still be in there." "God, don't tell me that goose couldn't get out in time," said Ben O'Sullivan.

With that, a figure came dashing through the cloud of smoke in the doorway carrying what seemed to be a dead body. "For God's sake, call an ambulance," Jimmy shouted as he laid Mrs Bourke down on her back and proceeded to blow into her mouth and press on her chest in an attempt to revive her. His actions were so composed and measured that all those around him felt inadequate to help. They had seen such rescues on "Baywatch" but this was for real, a local boy fighting for the life of a neighbour, and they were frozen in gaze at his actions as if spell-bound.

After about eight attempts to resuscitate her, Mrs Bourke finally let a cough that broke the silence and seemed to give people leave to move and talk again. Soon a fire brigade and ambulance arrived. The fire was extinguished and Mrs Bourke was rushed to hospital.

That night Jimmy McCarthy became a celebrity in Towtheline. "Hey, what you did was cool, real cool," said Ben O'Sullivan as he shook his hand. "Thanks Ben" replied Jimmy with a smile, but somewhere in the back of his mind he wondered, did Ben really understand what "REAL COOL" really meant.

My funny friend

by Sabrina Lynch

St Mary's College, Derry/Londonderry
2nd Prize
1996

My funny friend lives, breathes, walks and talks. She is called Dopey. The reason she is called Dopey is because she is dopey or in other words humorously stupid. I would describe Dopey to you as a clown because she acts like one and dresses like one. The trousers that Dopey wears are so big that I would fit into them THREE TIMES. Her shirt is long and a bit big on her but she tells me that it fits her perfect. Dopey acts so stupid, every word that she says is stupid. She doesn't think before she speaks. When I brought a few of my friends round to my house Dopey was in, me and my friends were watching TV when Dopey told my friends to stop watching TV because she owned it. I didn't think it was funny at all but all my friends found it very funny. They found it so funny that they couldn't speak. Tattered strands of mahogany hair fell down over her face. Dopey walks with a limp so it takes her a long time to walk just a short distance. The reaction that Dopey gets is fabulous because anyone who knows her finds her very amusing. Dopey can get on with anyone even if she doesn't like them, she is still courteous and friendly towards them, but I like Dopey most of all because she is my best friend.

Waiting

by Gavin Daly

St Killian's National School,
Crossreagh, Co Cavan
Highly Commended
1996

I waited for the boat to come in with a catch of fish,
looking down as the shimmering reflection
washes up against the pier.
Quiet and still the sea washes against the rocks,
hoping to shatter them.
Smells sent
Swivel up across the harbour of salty salty water
and dead fish.
The noise of the horn sounded
sending the birds flying.
Jimmy calls me to gut with him.
Seabirds pleading,
Waiting for us to throw out
the waste.

My music has a secret

by Ruth Gillan

Limavady High School, Limavady, Co Derry/Londonderry
1st Prize
1996

BANG! My bedroom door slammed as I sulked and shouted, "I hate this house!" I had to drown out the commotion downstairs, so I flicked on the radio and turned the volume to maximum. There! That would show them!

As my breathing slowed down, the music began to register in my mind. It was instrumental, the kind which allows you to day-dream with no words to disturb your thoughts. I had heard this piece of music before and now as I listened, my mind drifted back to that first time when I had heard it. . .

My parents had organised a picnic and told us only that we were going to have a long drive ahead of us. A long drive for me usually meant Belfast, so I concluded that was where we were destined. I was glad to see Mum making not only chicken sandwiches, but ham, jam and cheese varieties as well. That meant she was trying to please us all. The day began to look promising. Things looked up even more when Dad arrived home from night-shift on time and even smiled at us as he changed. It was with high hopes that my brothers Steven and Michael, my sister Sarah and I climbed into the back seat of the car.

The drive turned out to be as long as Mum had told us and the monotonous purr of the engine lulled my siblings to sleep. Since that left me with no-one to talk to, I unwound my head-phones, slotted the new tape I had got for Christmas into my personal stereo and pressed the play button. I was wondering how long the batteries would last, remembering the advert with the fluffy yellow rabbits playing drums, when my eyes caught a flash of a large, square road sign, "WELCOME TO DONEGAL."

Now, this was a new experience for me. I had never been to Donegal before and, since it was much more interesting than visiting Belfast, I peered with more determination out the car window, as the instrumental music continued, as beautiful and atmospheric as ever.

At first it looked pretty much like Co Antrim, but gradually the landscape began to change. It became more and more rugged, the colours changing from green to purples and browns. Then the car started to chug, as if it was complaining about having to travel so far. We were now going up-hill and the road was winding around and around, like the snake on Aaron's rod that I had seen in my Bible story book. As the car swept out on the corners, I was able to catch a brief glimpse of the ocean, winking at me. It seemed too shy to show itself completely, especially to strangers from Co Antrim.

I was brought back to my senses by the creak of the hand–brake being pulled up tightly, and within seconds Steven, Sarah and Michael were out of the car and screaming for Dad to play football with them. I wandered immediately over to the edge of the cliff and sat down on the grass, my tape still playing in my ears. The music matched the scene before me perfectly, and I was glad of my head-phones. They allowed me to block out all sound from outside and concentrate completely on the scenery, the white swirling ocean and the swooping and gliding birds.

After lunch, Sarah asked to borrow my stereo and, with a little help from my mother, I agreed. Back on the cliff, I was looking at the same scene, but now I was hearing it as well. The waves now crashed against the cliff as well as swirled. The gulls now spoke to each other as well as glided. The whole thing reminded me of the opening pages of *The Iron Man*, my favourite novel. The more I listened to the birds, the more I thought I understood what they were saying to each other. Males and females discussed the best site for this year's nest. The female felt like a change. Others were deciding where to dive for dinner. Oddly, their voices became as musical as the music from my head-phones, especially when played against the harmony of the ocean.

"Ruth! Come downstairs this minute! And turn that radio O.F.F.!" It was my Mum's angry voice. Still sulking, I did as I was told. "What on earth's the matter with you? Why were you stomping around the house?" I wanted to tell her that she had disturbed my dreams, had disrupted my contentment. I wanted my family to stay as happy as they had been that day in Donegal, everyone in harmony, but I didn't. Instead I murmured,
"I was listening to my radio. My favourite song was on!"

The photograph

by Edele Doherty

St John's Primary School, Derry/Londonderry

Highly Commended

1996

The room, the cradle where my mother first rocked me,
As I slowly drifted to sleep.
How she lulled so softly and smiled at me
With her gentle, brown eyes.
Beside her stands a tall, proud man – my father.
Close by, smiling in adoration
Four people – my grandparents.

I am made up of tales of
How my mother gave birth to my sisters
And cared for us with love.
Of how my parents brought us up
And taught us life skills.

Yes, I am made up of many tales,
Of an uncle who emigrated to Australia,
Of an English grandfather who came
and settled in Ireland,
Of an uncle who died shortly after birth,
And of a great grandmother who died in childbirth.

And I am here to carry these tales
And spread them to my children
So that the history of my family
May live on for years to come.